LEVEL
2

Night Sky

Stephanie Warren Drimmer

NATIONAL
GEOGRAPHIC

Washington, D.C.

For Dad, who looks up and wonders with me —S.W.D.

Published by National Geographic Partners, LLC, Washington, D.C. 20036. All rights reserved. Reproduction in whole or in part without written permission of the publisher is prohibited.

Library of Congress Cataloging-in-Publication Data

Names: Drimmer, Stephanie Warren, author. | National Geographic Society (U.S.)
Title: Night sky / Stephanie Warren Drimmer.
Description: Washington, DC : National Geographic, [2017] | Series: National geographic readers | Audience: Ages 5-8. | Audience: K to grade 3.
Identifiers: LCCN 2016051334 (print) | LCCN 2016053551 (ebook) | ISBN 9781426328152 (pbk. : alk. paper) | ISBN 9781426328169 (hardcover : alk. paper) | ISBN 9781426328176 (e-book) | ISBN 9781426328183 (e-book + audio)
Subjects: LCSH: Astronomy--Juvenile literature. | Stars--Juvenile literature.
Classification: LCC QB46 .D776 2017 (print) | LCC QB46 (ebook) | DDC 520--dc23
LC record available at https://lccn.loc.gov/2016051334

The publisher and author gratefully acknowledge the expert content review of this book by Dr. Laurance R. Doyle, director of the Institute for the Metaphysics of Physics at Principia College and lead research scientist of the Quantum Astrophysics Group at the SETI Institute, and the literacy review of this book by Mariam Jean Dreher, professor of reading education, University of Maryland, College Park.

Photo Credits

Cover (CTR), Landolfi Larry/Getty Images; header (UP), Deniss Ivenkovs/Shutterstock; vocab (THROUGHOUT), Oleksandr Yuhlchek/Shutterstock; 1 (CTR), YouraPechkin/Getty Images; 3 (LO RT), Torian/Shutterstock; 4¬–5 (CTR), Andrey Prokhorov/Shutterstock; 6 (LO), Rolf Nussbaumer Photography/Alamy Stock Photo; 7 (UP), Quaoar/Shutterstock; 8 (CTR), Mihai Andritoiu/Alamy Stock Photo; 9 (UP), Danny-photo80/Dreamstime; 10 (UP), Andrew McInnes/Alamy Stock Photo; 11 (UP), Jerry Schad/Science Source; 11 (LO), fluidworkshop/Shutterstock; 12–13 (CTR), Novarc Images/Alamy Stock Photo; 14 (UP), vchal/Shutterstock; 15 (LO), Library of Congress/Science Photo Library; 16 (UP), isak55/Shutterstock; 17 (CTR), shooarts/Shutterstock; 18 (UP), Jurik Peter/Shutterstock; 18 (CTR), CFimages/Alamy Stock Photo; 18 (LO), Torian/Shutterstock; 19 (UP), Triff/Shutterstock; 19 (CTR LE), Ditty_about_summer/Shutterstock; 19 (CTR RT), creativemarc/Shutterstock; 19 (LO), Andrey Armyagov/Shutterstock; 20–21 (CTR), Atlas Photo Bank/Science Source; 22 (UP), Walter Pacholka, Astropics/Science Source; 23 (LO), David Aguilar; 24–25 (CTR), Laurent Laveder/Science Photo Library; 26–27 (LO), BSIP/Science Source; 27 (UP), John Davis/Stocktrek Images/Science Source; 28 (LE), NASA; 30 (UP), godrick/Shutterstock; 30 (CTR), Detlev van Ravenswaay/Science Source; 30 (LO), Allexxandar/Shutterstock; 31 (UP), Atlas Photo Bank/Science Source; 31 (CTR RT), Frank Zullo/Science Source; 31 (CTR LE), BSIP/Science Source; 31 (LO), John R. Foster/Science Source; 32 (UP LE), Detlev van Ravenswaay/Science Photo Library; 32 (UP RT), jordache/Shutterstock; 32 (CTR LE), Konrad Wothe/Alamy Stock Photo; 32 (CTR RT), BISP/Science Source; 32 (LO LE), vovan/Shutterstock; 32 (LO RT), Andrey Armyagov/Shutterstock

**National Geographic supports K–12 educators with ELA Common Core Resources.
Visit natgeoed.org/commoncore for more information.**

Printed in the United States of America
17/WOR/1

Table of Contents

Look Up!

When the sun goes down, dots of light fill the night sky.

Some of them move. Others are still. Some twinkle. Others don't.

Have you ever wondered what they are?

Earth's Sidekick

On most nights, one object looks bigger and brighter than everything else. It's the moon.

The moon is a ball of rock that orbits Earth. It looks so big and bright because it's only about 240,000 miles from Earth. Compared with other objects in the night sky, that's pretty close!

Sky Word

ORBIT: To move in a path around another object in space

Sometimes, the moon looks like a circle. Other times, it's a curved sliver. That's because of the moon's orbit.

full moon

new moon

It takes the moon about one month to travel all the way around Earth. At the full moon, the side facing Earth is fully lit up by the sun. At the new moon, the side facing away from Earth is lit up.

Light from the sun reflects off the moon, making it look bright. As the moon orbits Earth, we see different amounts of the lit-up side. This makes the moon appear to change shape.

Sky Word

REFLECT: To bounce back from a surface

a lunar eclipse over Perth, Australia

Sometimes as the moon orbits, Earth lines up between the sun and the full moon. When that happens, Earth blocks most of the sun's light from reaching the moon. The moon looks dark orange red. This is called a lunar (LOO-nur) eclipse (ee-KLIPS).

a solar eclipse seen from northern Oregon, U.S.A.

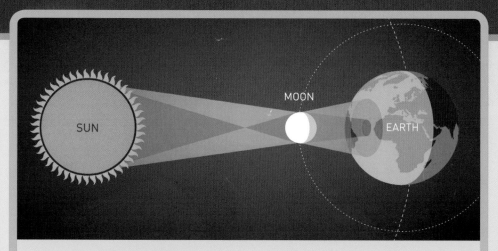

SUN

MOON

EARTH

Solar Eclipse

There are two types of eclipses: lunar and solar. In a solar eclipse, the moon lines up between the sun and Earth. The moon blocks sunlight from reaching part of Earth. To people in that spot on Earth, it looks like the sun has gone dark.

Twinkle, Twinkle

On a clear night, the sky is filled with tiny, twinkling lights. These twinkling lights are stars.

Stars are giant balls of burning gas. But since they are so far away, they look very small. Stars appear to twinkle because their light is bent back and forth as it travels through Earth's atmosphere (AT-mus-feer).

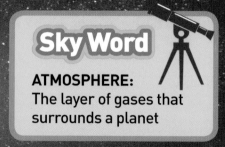

Sky Word

ATMOSPHERE:
The layer of gases that surrounds a planet

The Greeks called this constellation Orion. They imagined Orion was a great hunter holding a club and a lion's pelt.

If you connect stars with imaginary lines, you might see shapes in the sky. These are constellations (kon-stuh-LAY-shuns).

People have been looking for constellations since ancient times. Sailors used them to find their way across the seas. Storytellers made up tales about the people and animals they saw in the stars.

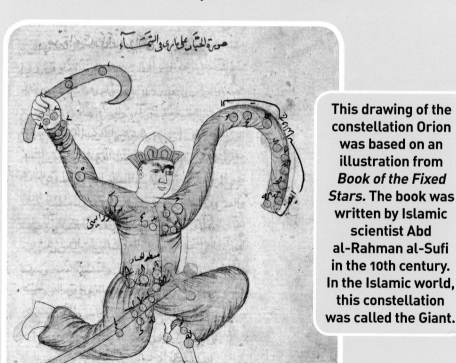

This drawing of the constellation Orion was based on an illustration from *Book of the Fixed Stars.* The book was written by Islamic scientist Abd al-Rahman al-Sufi in the 10th century. In the Islamic world, this constellation was called the Giant.

15

The Big Dipper is one famous group of stars. It's part of a constellation called Ursa Major. To some people, it looks like a ladle. Others see a wagon, a cleaver, or a mother bear and her three cubs.

STARGAZING TIPS
- Choose a clear night.
- Get away from city lights.
- Bring a blanket. Lie back and get comfortable for the best view of the sky!

This star map shows constellations that can be seen from the southern half of Earth. The stars are connected by imaginary lines.

A star map or app can help you find other constellations.

7 COOL FACTS
About Space

1

If you look closely (binoculars help!), you'll see that stars come in many colors: white, blue, yellow, orange, and red.

2

Enough space dust and rock falls to Earth each month to fill an Olympic-size swimming pool.

3

Jupiter has 67 moons.

4 Many stars are so far away that it takes millions of years for their light to reach Earth.

5 If you could drive to the sun, the trip would take 177 years.

6 The universe is 13.8 billion years old.

7 Have you spotted a light moving slowly across the night sky? If it's flashing, it's probably an airplane. If it's not, it's a satellite.

Sky Word

SATELLITE: A man-made object that orbits Earth and sends back information

A Home for the Sun

There's one star you know very well. It's the sun. The sun— and everything that orbits it— is in the Milky Way galaxy. Galaxies are large groups of stars held together by gravity.

Sky Word

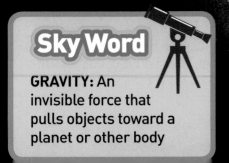

GRAVITY: An invisible force that pulls objects toward a planet or other body

There are 400 billion stars in the Milky Way. They form a giant spiral shape, as shown in this illustration.

You are here.

On a very clear night, you might see part of the Milky Way. It looks like a wide, hazy strip stretching across the sky.

Flying Objects

If you watch the sky for an hour on a clear night, you might see two or three meteors (MEE-tee-urz).

Have you ever seen a shooting star? These streaks of light aren't really stars. They're meteors—small lumps of rock that fall toward Earth. They glow as they quickly burn up in Earth's atmosphere.

Once in a while, you might also spot a bright, starlike object with a long tail. That's a comet. Watch for many nights, and you'll see that it travels slowly across the sky.

Comets are big chunks of ice and dust that orbit the sun. They are as big as a few miles across. When the sun's heat melts some of the ice away, a tail forms.

23

Spot the Dots

Jupiter

Stars twinkle in the night sky. But you may see some dots that don't. These are planets in our solar system. They are brighter than most stars.

Planets are large balls of rock, metal, or gas that orbit a star. Planets don't make their own light. They reflect light from the stars they orbit.

Venus

The planets in our solar system don't appear to twinkle because they are much closer to Earth than stars.

Besides Earth, seven other planets orbit our sun. You can spot some with just your eyes. Venus is the brightest, then Jupiter. Mars looks red. You can see Mercury and Saturn, too.

These are the eight planets of our solar system.
(Note: This illustration is not drawn to scale.)

Mars

Venus

Earth

Mercury

Jupiter

Visitors can view the night sky through this big telescope at the Three Rivers Foundation education center in Texas, U.S.A.

Uranus and Neptune are so far away that you need a telescope to see them.

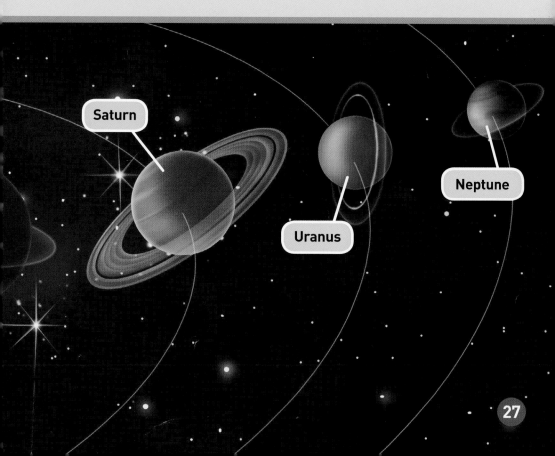

Saturn

Uranus

Neptune

Who's Out There?

Since 2012, NASA's Curiosity rover has been exploring Mars for signs of past or current life.

There are more than 300 billion trillion stars in space. That's a big number!

About half of the stars have planets. And scientists say that one of them could be home to living things, just like Earth.

When you stare at the night sky, someone might be staring back!

QUIZ WHIZ

How much do you know about the night sky? After reading this book, probably a lot! Take this quiz and find out.

Answers are at the bottom of page 31.

1

The moon is a ball of _____.

A. rock
B. fire
C. ice
D. gas

2

What color is the moon during a lunar eclipse?

A. bright white
B. pale yellow green
C. dark orange red
D. light blue

What do people think the constellation Ursa Major looks like?

A. a ladle
B. a wagon
C. a mother bear and her cubs
D. all of the above

3

What shape is the Milky Way?
A. a triangle
B. a spiral
C. a square
D. a star

4

What can you do for better stargazing?

A. Get away from city lights.
B. Choose a clear night.
C. Lie back on a blanket.
D. all of the above

5

6

Which planet do you need a telescope to spot?

A. Neptune
B. Venus
C. Mars
D. Jupiter

7

How many stars are there in space?

A. 300 million
B. 300 billion
C. 300 trillion
D. 300 billion trillion

ATMOSPHERE: The layer of gases that surrounds a planet

GRAVITY: An invisible force that pulls objects toward a planet or other body

LUNAR: Having to do with the moon

ORBIT: To move in a path around another object in space

REFLECT: To bounce back from a surface

SATELLITE: A man-made object that orbits Earth and sends back information